My Sl Words

Consultants
Ashley Bishop, Ed.D.
Sue Bishop, M.E.D.

Publishing Credits
Dona Herweck Rice, *Editor-in-Chief*
Robin Erickson, *Production Director*
Lee Aucoin, *Creative Director*
Sharon Coan, *Project Manager*
Jamey Acosta, *Editor*
Rachelle Cracchiolo, M.A.Ed., *Publisher*

Image Credits
cover and p.2 Erdosain/Bigstock; p.3 jordache/Shutterstock; p.4 Timmary/Shutterstock; p.5 Andre Blais/Shutterstock; p.6 jcooper342/Bigstock; p.7 maska/Shutterstock; p.8 ARENA Creative/Shutterstock; p.9 Gina Sanders/Shutterstock; p.10 WilleeCole/Shutterstock; back cover ARENA Creative/Shutterstock

Teacher Created Materials
5301 Oceanus Drive
Huntington Beach, CA 92649-1030
http://www.tcmpub.com
ISBN 978-1-4333-3982-0
© 2012 Teacher Created Materials, Inc.
Printed in China WAI002

Look at the slide.

Where is the slide?

Look at the sleeves.

Where are the **sl**eeves?

Look at the sling.

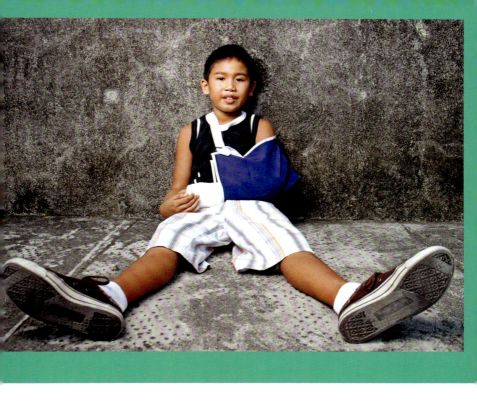

Where is the **sl**ing?

Look at the slug.

Where is the slug?

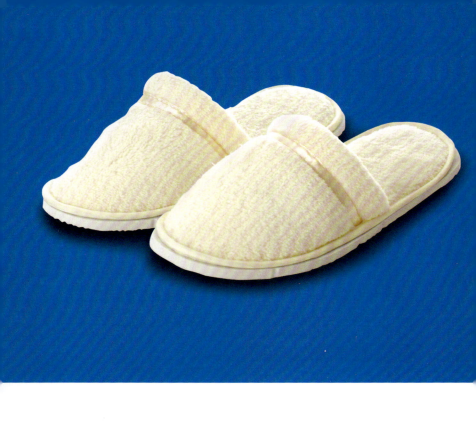

Look at the slippers.

Glossary

sleeves

slide

sling

slippers

slug

Sight Words

Look   at   the   Where   is   are

Activities

- Read the book aloud to your child, pointing to the *sl* words. Help your child describe where the *sl* objects are found.

- Visit a local park and have your child slide down a slide. To introduce more *sl* words, talk about how the slide is a slope or how it is slippery when wet.

- Have a family slumber party. Have each family member wear his or her favorite slippers. You may wish to draw pictures of slippers instead.

- Observe slugs outside your house. Have your child try moving like a slug, lying on his or her stomach and inching across the floor.

- Help your child think of a personally valuable word to represent the letters *sl*, such as *sleep*.